SOUTH CAMPUS

P9-ELW-576

LYONS T.H.S. LIBRARY
LA GRANGE, ILLINOIS

Escape

Teens Who Escaped the Holocaust to Freedom

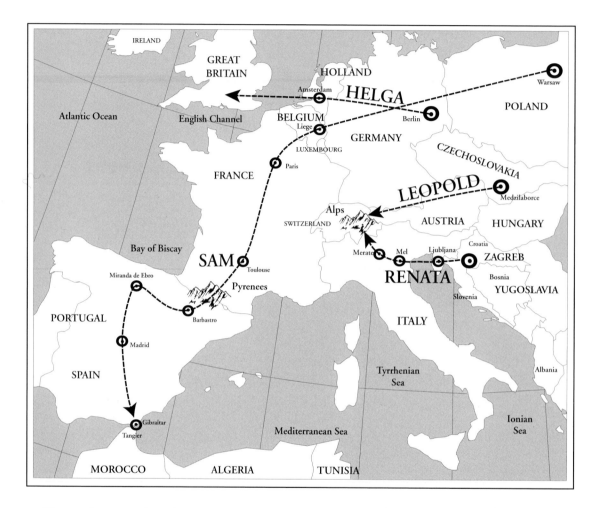

Those Jews fortunate enough to escape from the Nazis took many different escape routes. Above are the routes taken by Sam Cukier, Renata Markovic Eisen, Leopold Mendlovic, and Helga Edelstein Stummer.

SOUTH CAMPUS

940.53
Gi

Escape

Teens Who Escaped the Holocaust to Freedom

Sandra Giddens, M. Ed.

THE ROSEN PUBLISHING GROUP, INC.
NEW YORK

3 7424 50001 7453

LYONS T.H.S. LIBRARY
LA GRANGE, ILLINOIS

*Dedicated to my loving family, Owen, Justine, and Kyle
and, in loving memory,
to those who perished in the Holocaust*

Published in 1999 by The Rosen Publishing Group, Inc.
29 East 21st Street, New York, New York 10010

Copyright © 1999 by The Rosen Publishing Group, Inc.

All rights reserved. No part of this book may be reproduced in any form without permission in wiriting from the publisher, except by a reviewer.

First Edition

Library of Congress Cataloging-in-Publication Data

Giddens, Sandra.
    Escape : teens who escaped the Holocaust to freedom / Sandra Giddens.
       p.   cm. — (Teen witnesses to the Holocaust)
    Includes bibliographical references and index.
    Summary: Tells the stories of four teenagers who survived the horrors that the Nazis perpetrated on Jews during World War II.
    ISBN 0-8239-2843-8
    1. Jewish children in the Holocaust—Juvenile literature. 2. World War, 1939–1945—Jews—Rescue—Juvenile literature. [1. Holocaust survivors. 2. World War, 1939–1945—Jews.] I. Title. II. Series.
D804.6.G53 1999
940.53'18—dc21
                                          98-29009
                                             CIP
                                             AC

Manufactured in the United States of America

Contents

Introduction

It is important for everyone to learn about the Holocaust, the systematic murder of 6 million Jews during World War II (1939–1945). It is a dark scar across the face of human history. As a student, you are part of the future generation that will lead and guide the family of humankind. Your proper understanding of the Holocaust is essential. You will learn its lessons. You will be able to ensure that a Holocaust will never happen again and that the world will be a safe place for each person—regardless of his or her nationality, religion, or ethnicity.

Nazi Germany added a dangerous new element to the familiar concept of "dislike of the unlike." The Nazis introduced the idea that an *ethnic group* whom someone dislikes or hates can be isolated from the rest of the population and earmarked for total destruction, *without any possibility of survival.*

The Nazis chose the Jewish people for this fatal annihilation. Their definition of a Jew was a uniquely racial one: a person with Jewish blood. To the Nazis, a person with even one Jewish grandparent was a Jew—a person to be killed.

The Germans systematically rounded up Jews in the countries that they occupied during World War II. They built death camps equipped with the most sophisticated technology available in order to kill the Jews. With the assistance of collaborators (non-Germans who willingly helped), they murdered more than 6 million Jews. Among the victims were 1.5 million children and teenagers. These Jewish children, like Jewish adults, had no options. They were murdered because they had Jewish blood, and nothing they could do could change that.

Such a thing had never happened before in recorded history, despite the fact that genocide (deliberate destruction of people of one ethnic, political, or cultural group) had occurred. In the past, victims or oppressed people were usually offered an option to avoid death: they could change their religion, or be expelled to another country. But the Nazi concept of racism did not give the victim any possibility for survival, since a person cannot change his or her blood, skin color, or eye color.

A few non-Jewish people, known as the Righteous Among the Nations, saved Jews from death. They felt that they were their brothers' and sisters' keepers. But they were in the minority. The majority were collaborators or bystanders. During the Holocaust, I was a young child saved by several Righteous Poles. The majority of my family and the Jews of my town, many of whose families had lived there for 900 years, were murdered by the Nazis with the assistance of local collaborators. Photographs of those who were murdered gaze upon visitors to the Tower of Life exhibit that I designed for the United States Holocaust Memorial Museum in Washington, D.C.

We must learn the lessons of the Holocaust. We must learn to respect one another, regardless of differences in religion, ethnicity, or race, since we all belong to the family of humankind. The United States and Canada are both countries of immigrants, populated by many ethnic groups. In lands of such diversity, dislike of the unlike— the Nazi idea of using racial classification as a reason to destroy other humans—is dangerous to all of us. If we allow intolerance toward one group of people today, any of us could be part of a group selected for destruction tomorrow. Understanding and respecting one another regardless of religion, race, or ethnicity is essential for coexistence and survival.

In this book individuals who were teenagers during the Holocaust share their experiences of life before and during the war and of the days of liberation. Their messages about their families, friends, love, suffering, survival, liberation, and rebuilding of new lives are deeply inspiring. They are important because these survivors are among the last eyewitnesses, the last links to what happened during the Holocaust.

I hope that their stories will encourage you to build a better, safer future "with liberty and justice for all."

Yaffa Eliach Ph.D.
Professor of History and Literature,
Department of Judaic Studies, Brooklyn College

Background photo: Thumbprints from the identification papers of Sam Cukier, who fled to Spain to escape the Nazis.

chapter one

The Maze

Imagine yourself standing inside a maze, trying to find a way out. Imagine that no matter which direction you turn, a new wall appears, cutting off one of your escape routes. Each time you think you are on the right path the walls close in on you. Now suppose that you are told that if you leave the maze you will be worse off. Do you give up, or do you keep trying to escape?

Being a Jew in Europe during the 1930s was very much like stepping into a maze. On January 30, 1933, Adolf Hitler, the leader of the Nazi Party, became chancellor of Germany. Hitler had great power in Germany, and he hated the Jews. His plan was to make the world *Judenrein*, free of Jews.

Two months after becoming chancellor, on April 1, 1933, Hitler declared a daylong national boycott of Jewish stores and businesses in Germany. Three months after he came to power, the Nazis had created the Gestapo, or secret state police. Six months after he came to power, the only legal political party in Germany was the Nazi Party. All others had been banned. Political opponents had been arrested. Hitler's grip over Germany was firm. Without the Jews of Germany being aware of it, the entry to the Nazi maze was being closed behind them.

Throughout the 1930s, the rights of German Jews were gradually taken away. Some could foresee more trouble in the future. They left Germany,

German-Jewish teens fortunate enough to escape Germany in 1936 bid farewell to family and friends. Their destination was Palestine.

A Jewish-owned store in Berlin on the day of the anti-Jewish boycott. The sign reads, "Germans! Defend Yourselves! Do not buy from Jews!"

traveling to distant places such as the United States and Palestine (Israel today). They left the maze just in time. Others moved elsewhere in Europe, thinking they had escaped Hitler's reach. Most stayed, hoping and believing that the persecution and mistreatment by the Nazis would stop. It did not.

In September 1935, the German Reichstag, or parliament, enacted the Nuremberg Laws. These laws robbed German Jews of their citizenship. They made it illegal for Jews to marry Aryans, "pure-blooded" Germans.

The Nuremberg Laws and other laws isolated the Jews from the rest of the German population. Jewish children were expelled from schools. Jews had to have their official papers stamped with the letter "J." Men had to add Israel to their names and women had to add Sarah to show they were Jewish. Many Jews believed that these laws, as terrible as they were, were the worst thing that would happen. At least Germans and Jewish Germans would be able to continue living side by side.

But restrictions on Jews in Germany and in Austria, which was annexed by Germany in 1938, grew even harsher. By the beginning of 1939, a mass panic and departure of German and Austrian Jews occurred. Many moved east, especially to Poland, trying to escape. But the nations to which they fled would not always allow them to stay. Some

Background photo: Helga Edelstein's identity card, marked with the letter "J."

limited the number of Jews they would accept; others refused to allow any Jews to enter. Those who were turned away either had to figure out quickly where else to go or were forced to return home.

On March 15, 1939, German troops occupied part of Czechoslovakia. The Nazis began their abuse of Jews there as well. Six months later, on September 1, 1939, the Germans invaded Poland. World War II had begun. The Jews of Poland—including those who earlier had fled to Poland from Austria, Czechoslovakia, and Germany—tried to escape. But as German troops advanced, the walls of the maze were closing in on the Jews. Where could they go? Whom could they trust? Most were trapped.

In Poland, as in most of the nations Germany later occupied, the Nazis made the Jews wear a six-pointed star on their clothes. The Jews had to carry a Jewish identification card at all times. Beatings, shootings, public humiliation, and torture of the Jews were daily occurrences.

By the time most Jews realized that life under Nazi rule was intolerable, it was too late. Many tried to escape, but by now it was nearly impossible. At every turn in the maze, legal and bureaucratic barriers to Jews blocked formerly open pathways. Fear haunted each minute of every day. The Jewish people were being systematically rounded up and murdered.

The war in Europe lasted until May 8, 1945. Even on the last day Jews were being murdered. Six million Jews were killed in the Holocaust. Those who escaped did so against all odds.

Jews arrested in the Podgorze neighborhood of Cracow, Poland, are lined up on the street with their hands against the wall of a building, December 1939.

chapter two

In the Beginning

Helga, Leopold, Renata, and Sam are four survivors who escaped out of the maze to freedom. When World War II started Leopold was nineteen, Sam eighteen, Helga thirteen, and Renata eleven. Each had to travel under dangerous circumstances to gain freedom. They lost a great deal to be free: their homes, their childhood dreams, and often their families.

Helga

Helga Edelstein Stummer was born in Berlin, Germany. When she was twelve, just before the outbreak of World War II, Helga managed to flee to freedom. She recalls what life was like growing up in Nazi Germany in the 1930s.

I was born in Berlin on August 17, 1926. Berlin was a cosmopolitan city, which meant it was both modern and cultured. The Jews of Berlin were well integrated into the culture of Germany. Jews and non-Jews worked and lived together in communities.

Background photo: Helga and her sister Lotte.

My father was a very proud German citizen. He had fought in World War I for Germany, and he was a decorated soldier. In Berlin he had a thriving business as the manager of a large department store. My mother was wonderful. She was full of life. She was sixteen years younger than my father. My mother had time to share my childhood with me. When Mother was around, there was always laughter in the air.

We shared the house with my caring half-sister, Lotte, who later helped save my life. Also sharing our household was my loving grandmother. She came into our lives permanently in 1935 because my mother was very ill.

Berlin was the capital of Germany and known around the world for its culture and taste. Berlin street scene, 1930.

In 1936 the Nazi Party took away my father's job because he was a Jew. He soon became physically and emotionally exhausted. He could not understand what had happened to the Germany he once knew.

I remember 1937 very well. I was only eleven years old. My laughing mother would not share my life with me any longer. She died of cancer. My father seemed to age before my eyes. He appeared to be a broken man.

My biggest dream was that I would save the world from the evil man Hitler. I would stare at my reflection in my floor-length mirror and think of ways that I personally could destroy him. I would also dream that my mother would come back to me and we would live in a safe world and laugh together.

Leopold

Leopold Mendlovic was born in Medzilaborce, Czechoslovakia. At that time, many Czechoslovakian Jews were secular. But in Slovakia most Jews were observant and religious. For Slovakian Jews antisemitism was a part of life. The Zionist movement there was quite strong.

Leopold was nineteen when he escaped from the Nazis. He recalls what it was like growing up in Slovakia in the 1930s, before Czechoslovakia was invaded by Germany.

I came from a very large Orthodox family. We lived in a small town called Medzilaborce, Slovakia, which was part of Czechoslovakia. After World War I, democracy prospered in Czechoslovakia. The country was one of the most booming industrialized nations in Eastern Europe.

I was one of nine brothers and sisters. We lived in a close-knit Orthodox Jewish community of 200 families. My father provided for our family. He was a successful builder of houses. My mother was an incredible woman. Both my parents were loving and caring. Although we had a large family, we were all treated fairly and equally. In our Jewish community, it was felt that if you had anything to give, you would share it with families less fortunate than yours. The Jewish community took care of the poor among them to make sure they were able to lead decent lives.

I remember sitting at the dinner table and sharing our food with poor strangers. My mother would always give the same portion to everyone. It did not matter that she had nine children of her own to feed. I would sit at the table with these strangers and feel pity at how they dressed or how they smelled. My parents, on the other hand, were very accepting and never said a word.

Antisemitism was a way of life for me. The non-Jewish boys would constantly swear at me and other Jewish boys. We knew which corners to avoid. At home we were taught to be humane and to disregard people's differences. It was a puzzle to me: Why did people hate Jews?

In the 1930s, antisemitism was common in Slovakia. In Nazi Germany, it became part of classroom instruction. Above, two German Jews are humiliated in class. The words on the blackboard read, "The Jew is our greatest enemy! Beware of the Jews!"

As I grew up, I wanted to be a professional. I was leaning toward politics. As a teenager I admired democratic presidents, especially the president of Czechoslovakia. I was very headstrong and determined, and I always enjoyed a good debate. I had dreams and aspirations. I was going to succeed in this world.

Renata

Renata Eisen was born in Zagreb, Yugoslavia. At that time, Yugoslavia was a safe place for Jews to live, and many Jews belonged to the middle class. Before Hitler came to power antisemitism there was very limited compared to other places in Europe. As the persecution of Jews grew in Germany, however, antisemitism in Yugoslavia also intensified.

Renata fled from Zagreb when she was twelve, after the Nazis gained control of Croatia. She recalls her early life in Zagreb.

I was born Renata Markovic on October 2, 1929, in the town of Zagreb, Croatia. My father, a quiet and deeply religious man, was known as a reluctant talker. That left the talking and decision making to my

Children at the Jewish summer camp of the Morgenroyt schools in Romania, 1939. The Jews of Romania were rounded up and deported to death camps in 1944.

mother. Her "Never say no" attitude was essential in saving my life. My father had a factory that manufactured textiles, and my mother was in charge of the sales. I had two brothers and a sister. We were a caring family.

I came from an Orthodox home in a community where everyone knew everyone else's business. I remember an incident from when I was only seven and my sister was a teenager. She went to school one Saturday to take a test. This was taboo in an Orthodox neighborhood, because part of our religious practice was that we did not write or work on Shabbat. The community ostracized her. She had to leave our home and go to another school because of disobeying our religious *laws. My family learned that the power of the community was very strong.*

I remember being a bold, extremely happy child. I skipped rope, played marbles, and enjoyed being surrounded with friends and family. Reading was a passion for me. One of my favorite books was called The Boys from Paul Street. *It was about an underprivileged child being picked on by a gang of boys. Sadly, he died in the end.*

The yearning that started when I was very young and that never left me was to travel. I loved to read foreign novels. I would picture myself as the heroine in their exotic settings. I fell in love with an older cousin who was able to travel the world. He did not know that I existed, but the fact that he could travel everywhere and see everything was enticing to my young mind. Before I knew it, I was to start a journey that I would never forget.

Sam

Sam Cukier was born in Warsaw, Poland. At that time, Poland was the country with the largest population of Jews in Europe. In Poland were rich Jews, poor Jews, and middle-class Jews. Many were secular, and many others were observant. Some lived in cities, and some lived in *shtetls*—villages or small towns.

Sam left Poland when he was seventeen. He recalls what it was like growing up there in the 1930s.

I was born December 3, 1920, in Warsaw, the capital of Poland. People would often remark that the Jews of Warsaw were very strong-willed and determined. I know that I shared the same attitude. It was probably what saved my life.

My father was a merchant who taught me that it was always important to learn. My mother also encouraged education for both men

and women. She thought that women should take care of themselves, a modern idea in our Jewish community.

I had three sisters. My sister Regine was the strongest of us all. She knew what she wanted and always went after it. Sabina was just the opposite, always a gentle creature following my mother's recommendations. Unfortunately, my little sister Tobcia died when she was only five years old. She became very ill, and the house was put under quarantine. I was sent away. When I returned, my little sister was gone. This was my first introduction to losing someone I loved.

One summer when I was in high school, I went to a pre-military camp. Some other Jewish boys were there as well, but the majority of the camp was made up of Polish non-Jews. One tradition at this camp was that on the last day of camp the non-Jews beat up the Jews. This was an expected practice.

I went to bed that night, prepared to fight back. I even hid weapons under my pillow! But when the gang of ruffians came to get me, the Polish non-Jews of my tent protected me. I was one of their boys. I learned that there were Polish non-Jews I could trust. They learned that they could respect this one Jewish boy.

I was a reader and a keen student. Languages came very quickly to me. My motto in life was that each individual has to find what is best for him. It was expected in my home, as well as my dream, to go to university to study.

The university in Warsaw was known for its antisemitism. Jews were not readily accepted and were in danger of being beaten up, so generally, studies outside of Poland were more attractive. I applied to and was accepted into a university in Belgium. Although I could not have known it then, this decision affected the future course of my life.

chapter three

Preparing for the Escape

By summer 1938, circumstances in Germany were so terrible that an international conference, the Evian Conference, was held to discuss where the Jews of Germany and Austria could go for refuge. Despite the good intentions of many nations, only Britain agreed to allow Jews to immigrate in any large number.

On November 7, 1938, a young German Jew by the name of Hershel Grynszpan shot a high-ranking Nazi official in Paris. Two days later, his victim, Ernst vom Rath, died from the gunshot wound.

The Nazis used vom Rath's assassination as an excuse to stage a violent demonstration against the Jews throughout Germany and Austria. It became known as Kristallnacht, the night of broken glass. On the night of November 9–10, 1938, Nazi-organized mobs brutally smashed the windows of Jewish shops, set fire to synagogues, looted Jewish homes, and injured and murdered Jews. Thirty thousand Jews were taken away and sent to concentration camps.

After Kristallnacht, appeals were again made to the world for nations to open their borders, this time to rescue Jewish children in Germany and Austria. The United Kingdom was one of the only countries that opened its doors. It permitted 10,000 Jewish children and teenagers to enter Great Britain. The Nazis insisted on three conditions before the children could leave. The sum of £50 per

Herschel Grynszpan
was born in Hannover,
Germany, of parents who
were Polish Jews. In 1936,
Grynszpan moved from
Germany to France to study.
In November 1938, his
family and thousands of
other Polish Jews residing
in Germany were expelled
to Poland without warning.
The Poles would not accept
them. Lacking food and
crowded into pigsties and
other terrible lodgings, the
refugees lived a wretched

existence on the German-Polish border. On November
7, 1938, after learning of his family's fate,
Grynszpan gunned down Ernst vom Rath, the third
secretary of the German embassy in Paris. The
diplomat's death two days later gave the Nazi
leadership the justification it needed to unleash
Kristallnacht. In 1940 Grynszpan was turned over to
the Germans by pro-Nazi French authorities.

child (about $250 in 1938) had to be paid; the children had to be between three and seventeen years of age; and all children had to leave alone, without parents or adult family members. Some children had sponsors at the other end, some did not.

These special transports of children were called Kindertransports. When the children arrived they were scattered to foster homes, schools, farms, and orphanages all over England, Scotland, Wales, and Ireland. Most were separated from their brothers and sisters. More than 80 percent of these children never saw their families again because their family members had perished in the Holocaust.

Helga

Helga well remembers the events leading up to Kristallnacht, as well as the night itself.

The times were becoming very difficult for a Jewish person living in Berlin. We could sit only on yellow benches designated for Jews. Some newspapers exhibited antisemitic caricatures of Jews on their front pages. Billboards had signs that read "Get Out, Jews." The propaganda was very strong. Non-Jews whom we previously trusted began to treat us as second-class citizens.

Kristallnacht occurred when I was twelve. I remember the shattering of glass. I remember the fear that was all around. I went to Jewish school the next day and saw the burned-out shell of the synagogue that we had gone to every Saturday. My teacher was extremely nervous. He would say, "Get away from the windows." Only four children showed up for school that day. There were hushed whispers all around. Fathers and uncles had been rounded up and taken away, mostly during the day and some in the night. No one knew where they had gone. Everyone was too scared to talk, and this made me extremely nervous and on guard. For the first time since my mother's death I felt frightened. My world became unsafe.

Graffiti on he wall of a Jewish cemetery in Berlin reads, "The death of the Jews will end the Saarland's misery." It is indicative of the antisemitism that gripped Nazi Germany, 1933.

World War II started on September 1, 1939, when Germany invaded Poland. By that time, the Kindertransports had stopped running. Jewish groups tried to collect money to send fleeing refugees to Palestine. Traveling to Palestine was extremely difficult and dangerous.

In 1939, a ship named the *S.S. St. Louis* sailed from Germany with 937 Jewish refugees. It was bound for Havana, Cuba. When it arrived in port, it was unable to land. The Cuban government would not accept the Cuban visas the refugees had previously paid for to gain entry into Cuba. It was a political football match played between the Cuban politicians at the expense of the Jews. The Jews lost. After six days in port, they were turned away.

The *S.S. St. Louis* sailed north to Miami, Florida, where the U.S. Coast Guard would not allow it to dock. Telegrams were sent to President Roosevelt asking him to allow the refugees to land and to First Lady Eleanor Roosevelt requesting that the children be permitted

to land. But the Jews on the
S.S. St. Louis were not allowed to
enter the United States. Canada
would not let the passengers disem-
bark, either.

The ship, with its discouraged
passengers, was forced to sail back across
the Atlantic. Finally Belgium, the
Netherlands, France, and England agreed to
take in the refugees. But because three of those
countries were later occupied by the Nazis, three-

European Jewish refugees aboard the *S.S. St. Louis* look out through
the porthole of the ship while it is docked in the port of Havana.

After returning to Europe, *S.S. St. Louis* Captain Gustav Schroeder
negotiates landing permits for some of the passengers in the port of
Antwerp, Belgium, June 1939.

quarters of the Jews who had been passengers on the *S.S. St. Louis* were
later murdered in the Holocaust.

In the meantime, Germany continued to conquer many nations. By
1941, the Jews had nowhere to go. They were caught in the maze.

Some countries and individuals did try to save Jews. Spain had
friendly relations with Germany during the war. Yet the Spaniards were
helpful in saving more than 40,000 Jews by allowing them to cross their
borders or claim Spanish citizenship (and Spanish protection) if they
could trace their roots back to Spain. Italy was allied with Germany, yet
many Italians tried to save Jews. Japan, another German ally, saved
thousands of Jews by letting them immigrate to Shanghai, China,
which Japan ruled at the time. Some Jews fled to Russia and survived.

In the Netherlands, many people tried to hide Jews and give
them protection. The citizens of Denmark, which was occupied by
the Germans, nonetheless arranged the miraculous transportation
of some 7,000 Jewish men, women, and children—almost the entire
Jewish population of Denmark—to Sweden, which opened its
borders to them. Finland also protected its Jewish population. Raoul
Wallenberg, a Swedish diplomat in Hungary, managed to save
100,000 Hungarian Jews. But these were the exceptions.

Raoul Wallenberg was a Swedish diplomat who saved the lives of tens of thousands of Jews in Budapest. In spring 1944, the Nazis deported Jews from provincial Hungary. In July 1944, with the support of the American War Refugee Board,  the Swedish Foreign Ministry sent Wallenberg to Budapest to help protect the thousands of Jews who remained in the Hungarian capital. Wallenberg issued thousands of official Swedish protective passes to Jews and established a network of thirty-one protected houses for them in the capital. When the Soviet army liberated Budapest in January 1945, nearly 100,000 Jews were still alive in Budapest. Wallenberg was detained by Soviet agents and was never heard from again.

Leopold

Leopold remembers the terrifying order from the pro-Nazi Slovakian government for young unmarried Jewish men and women to be taken from his town and the surrounding towns to work camps.

On March 14, 1939, Hitler made Slovakia an independent state. It became a satellite of Germany, and a pro-Nazi government was established in Slovakia.

The Slovaks were as bad as the Germans in their antisemitism and thoroughly enjoyed giving Jews humiliating jobs. In spring

1940, they gave me the job of cleaning up the excrement of the horses from the street and sweeping it into buckets.

March 1942 was the scariest time of my life. There was a decree for all the young people of working age to report to the town square the next day. The authorities pretended that the youths were going to work camps in Poland. By that time we knew what was happening in Poland. We knew that Jews were being mass-murdered. We knew of the concentration camps where people of all ages were being gassed.

That night my three brothers, Manes, Majer, Nandor, and I crossed the small river near our house and hid in the woods. The water was freezing. Our pants were frozen to our flesh. We shivered all through the night and prayed that we would not be picked up by the pro-Nazi Slovaks, who were neighbors, people we knew.

In the middle of the night we heard the screams. We separated in order to increase our

By 1942, word had traveled to Slovakia that Jews were being worked to death and killed in concentration camps like this one in Mauthausen, Austria.

Austrian Nazis and local residents look on as Jews are forced to get on their hands and knees and scrub the pavement. Vienna, Austria, 1938.

chance of not being discovered. Manes, my brother, was hiding in another part of the forest, maybe 300 feet (100 m) away. He was picked up by Slovak border guards who were looking for escapees. He was shipped to Auschwitz.

Together the remainder of my family hid in the attic of one of our relatives. We waited until the roundup was over, when the pro-Nazi Slovaks would stop looking for people. Then we made it home to safety.

After that, my brothers and I never went outside. Anytime there was a suspicious person lurking around the house, we hid in a crawl space under the trapdoor. This is how we lived for three months, until June 1942.

The rumor around our town was that there was going to be another deportation, this time of Jews of all ages. My brothers and I planned to hide in the forest again. My mother and father were in

*their fifties and thought they needed an alternative plan. One of our
friendly Slovak neighbors promised he would take good care of my
parents. They brought all their belongings over to his house. That
night we had a brief moment to say good-bye to our parents before
we ran off into the woods. My parents went to hide next door in our
neighbor's attic.*

*Our uncle told us the terrible truth the following day. That kind
Slovak neighbor turned my loving parents in at four o'clock in the
morning. He actually notified the authorities that they were hiding
in his attic. My parents were murdered in the gas chambers of
Auschwitz. I never saw them again.*

*My brothers and I then went to hide in my uncle's house. He had
connections with the Slovak authorities, but not enough to do anything about my parents. I remember 1942 as the time I stayed hidden!
One day in September 1942 I had to use the outhouse in back of my
uncle's home. A Slovak policeman saw me and started chasing me. I
tried to climb a fence with barbed wire on top. I got caught and felt
my flesh being torn away. I was taken to police headquarters, where
my uncle knew whom to bribe to get me released.*

*In the meantime, Polish Jews fleeing Poland were crossing into
Slovakia. They confirmed our worst fears: it was only going to get
worse. I knew that I had to escape.*

In May 1940 the Auschwitz concentration camp was established.
On September 3, 1941, the toxic gas Zyklon B was first used at
Auschwitz to murder Jews. The Nazis had developed an efficient
killing machine. The year 1941 brought daily reminders that Jews
were not safe in Europe.

Renata

The situation became progressively worse for Renata and her family in
Zagreb, Croatia. In 1941 they decided to escape.

Background photo: In 1941, the Nazis began executing Jews
in newly occupied areas of the Soviet Union rather than sending them
to death camps. Above, German police and pro-Nazi Ukrainians look on
as Jewish women are forced to undress just before they are killed,
Sniatyn, Poland, 1942.

On April 10, 1941, the Germans bombed Belgrade, the capital of Serbia, and the city fell on April 13. Then the Germans marched into Zagreb. I was only eleven years old. I remember feeling two emotions. The first was sheer panic watching the troops and tanks. They would march in circles through our town over and over to intimidate us. It worked! Second, I was confused because my Croatian friends who were not Jewish would not play with me anymore in the courtyard.

Since the start of the war, we had heard rumors about Jewish people being taken to concentration camps but did not know what was happening there. We thought they were work camps.

In May 1941, two Croatian policemen came to our apartment to deliver a letter. It said that both my brothers had to report for work camp in a couple of days. All the Jewish families in Zagreb received this kind of letter concerning their older sons. Many families appeared not to be concerned. They thought it was like a summer camp and that a little work never hurt anyone! They were buying flashlights and packing their boys' bags.

My mother was very uncomfortable with this proposition. Her gut feeling told her to escape to Italy. But the rest of the Orthodox community shunned her.

A gas mask and containers of Zyklon B poison gas pellets, used at the death camp at Majdanek, Poland, were found when the camp was liberated.

They said, "You will make trouble for all of us if you leave." I suppose after seeing what the community had done to her daughter for violating Shabbat, she remained silent.

All 210 boys in our community were taken. Two boys were allowed to stay due to my mother. When they read out the edict saying all boys born between 1921 and 1923 had to go to camp, my mother pointed out that my younger brother was born in 1924. They agreed to let my younger brother and one other boy leave. My mother could not save my older brother.

For the next month or so, we received postcards from my brother. In July there was silence. After the war we heard the true story, an eyewitness account. That summer all 210 boys were lined up at the top of a ravine and shot. I can never get the picture out of my mind of my gentle brother falling, never to breathe again.

Renata and her older sister.

That summer the pro-Nazi Croatians took over our apartment and we moved in with my maternal grandmother. On the day of the move my sister was taken away by the Croatian police (Ustashi). My mother bribed anyone and everyone to get her released from the police station.

She was set free. My mother sent her to Hungary to be safe, but sadly she was not. My quiet sister was eventually rounded up and taken to Auschwitz in a cattle car. Somehow she survived there, but the atrocities she had witnessed left her emotionally a shell.

In August a German commander was installed at my parents' factory. My mother felt that all men were in danger, so my brother and father left, escaping to Italy.

Now all that was left of the immediate family was my grandmother, my mother, and I. My mother was still feeling she had the responsibility of running the factory and she had my grandmother and me to protect. In late September I saw two policemen across the street, knocking on the door of my grandmother's house, where my mother and I also lived. My cousin ran to the factory to tell my mother. She told me to take my grandmother and meet my mother at a friend's house outside of Zagreb. My grandmother would not go with me. That was the last I saw of her.

Apparently my sister and my grandmother ended up on the same transport to Auschwitz. My sister recalls hearing my grandmother screaming hysterically, almost as if she had gone insane. My grandmother was taken in the line to be gassed the first day.

Sam

Sam's luck stayed with him throughout the war years. Each step along his journey saw him constantly getting out just in the nick of time.

In November 1938, I left for Liège, Belgium, to go to university. I had to obtain a Polish passport and student visa to Belgium. It was not easy but I finally left legally. I was studying to be a chemical engineer. In the spring of 1939, I wrote to my family that I would come home for a visit during summer vacation. My father was very emphatic, stating that I should stay where I was, so I remained in Belgium. The war started in September 1939, and in May 1940, the Germans came to Belgium. I knew that I had to escape. I left just in time.

On Friday, May 10, 1940, I took an attaché case and left on the train for France. I was one of 50,000 Jews that fled Belgium in May. I thought that if I got out of Belgium, I would be able to join the armed forces. My first stop was Paris. I wanted to protect my family

New arrivals to Auschwitz saw the sign that deceptively claimed "Work will make you free." Most were gassed within minutes or hours of their arrival.

by fighting. I was admitted to the Polish army stationed in France.

Within days the Germans invaded France and overpowered the French army. The Polish officers in my unit fled to England, leaving the soldiers behind. I knew that I had to escape again. Along the roads, with thousands of other people desperately trying to avoid the conquering troops, I walked and hitchhiked to the south of France. I aimed for Toulouse for safety because it was still a free zone, not yet occupied by the Germans.

For two years I received some letters through the Red Cross from my family, and then silence. Little did I know until after the war was over that my mother and Sabina had been rounded up in 1942 and sent to their deaths in Treblinka. After the war, I also learned that my

Background photo: Eyeglasses and other belongings were taken from Jews (for use by Germans) before they were gassed at Auschwitz.

father was killed in 1943 fighting in the Warsaw Ghetto Uprising.

If I had delayed, I might never have been able to cross the border to Spain. Jews were being picked up in France and were being sent to concentration camps. I had to escape. I knew that I was determined to survive.

For twenty-eight days, residents of the Warsaw ghetto fought the Nazis with limited weapons but fierce determination. Most were later deported to death camps. Warsaw, Poland, May 16, 1943.

Opposite: German troops invade Paris and march past the Arc de Triomphe.

chapter four

The Escape

After Kristallnacht there was an attempted mass exodus to get out of Germany. In Berlin, Helga was able to get on a Kindertransport.

Helga

My father was in a state of shock after Kristallnacht. He was a man of age fifty-nine. The destruction of buildings and people all around him left him silent and fearful. My grandmother also was very old and was trying to be strong for all of us. Lotte, my older sister, was the only one working on getting me out before it was too late.

Lotte left in December 1938 to go to England to work as a maid. In order for me to leave she had to find a guarantor. A guarantor was someone who would put up the money and assume responsibility for the children that were coming to them on the Kindertransport. Lotte had sent a picture of me sitting on top of a mermaid statue to my guarantor. They agreed to take me in.

On July 4, 1939, the train was waiting for me. I said good-bye to my wonderful grandmother at our home and my father took me to the station. I remember being happy to leave. It seemed to be an adventure. I never thought that this would be the last time I would see my father and grandmother.

I was heading off in another direction, and I was looking forward to it. The train pulled away from the station. My father was waving. He was a distant image by the tracks. And then he was gone.

We were told by the leaders on the train to be quiet and watch our comments until we crossed to Holland. One never knew if the border crossing would go smoothly. Many of the younger children did not understand. We did not recognize the signs of danger. The older teenagers and adults knew the risks being taken.

After the train we traveled on an English boat. When we landed, all the children had to sit in a big room like a gymnasium and wait to be picked up by our guarantors. We would whisper together when a person arrived and say, "Hope that is not my lady, I do not like the looks of her." When it was my turn, this woman appeared. She was just the opposite of my fashionable, laughing mother! She was with Lotte so I knew it was my turn to say good-bye to all the children of the Kindertransport.

I did not get along very well in my new home. I was a teenage girl and they did not understand me. I had to bicycle four miles every day to school. Then when I got home I had to do chores. I never had friends over. Sometimes I traveled great distances to be with my friends. It was mainly a lonely life. My sister was living somewhere else so we could only write to each other.

Background photo: Members of the first Kindertransport arrive in Harwich, England, on December 2, 1938.

39

In order to hear about my father and grandmother, we arranged to write letters through a good friend who lived in Belgium. I still have the beautiful German letters that my grandmother wrote me. She loved me very much and wished me only the best that life could offer. She also had to write to tell me that on March 2, 1940, my father died. Maybe after losing so much and the terrible war raging on, he just gave up on living. All I knew was that my grandmother was left behind all by herself. I was orphaned at thirteen.

The letters from Belgium stopped coming. I heard that my grandmother was picked up and sent to a concentration camp. Did she die along the way? Was she gassed in a concentration camp? Were they cruel to her before she died? She could hardly walk.

The people that took me in had more bad news for me. They were sending me elsewhere. I was moved thirteen times in the thirteen years that I was in England, for many reasons. For instance, one of my sponsors was in ill health, and later I had to be evacuated for the purposes of getting away from the bombing. I learned to adapt very easily.

Thirteen-year-old Helga at a carnival near London, 1939.

I treasured my grandmother's letters, as they provided me with warmth and love when I was moved from place to place.

Like Helga, some teens and children fled from the Nazis on the Kindertransports. Others escaped alone or with a few other people. Often they attempted to flee using routes that were uncertain at best. Their escape was complicated by the fact that German troops were invading and bombing most of the nations of Europe.

An omnibus and building damaged by a nighttime German bombing raid on London, 1940.

Reinhard Heydrich (1904–1942) was head of the
Nazi Intelligence Service and later of the Reich
Central Security Office. He had vast control
over the fate of those considered enemies of the
Nazis. From 1939 on he headed the implementation
of Nazi anti-Jewish policy. On September 21,
1939, he ordered the creation of Jewish ghettos.
On January 20, 1942, he convened the Wannsee
Conference to discuss the details of the Final
Solution—the plan to kill all the Jews of
Europe. Later, he oversaw its implementation.
On May 27, 1942, Heydrich was killed in an
ambush near Prague, Czechoslovakia, by Czech
resistance fighters working with the British.

Opposite: Norwich, England, burns after a German
bombing raid, June 2, 1941.

Leopold

Leopold had lost most of his family, escaped a deportation, been arrested, and been freed. He now took desperate measures.

Trains regularly carried coal from Slovakia to Switzerland. It was rumored that some people hid in the coal trains. It was a chance. My brother Nandor and I decided that we would use this as our escape route. We also went with my uncle's daughter, her husband, and their six-year-old child. We paid a broker to sneak us onto the train. It was December 21, 1942. We took dry toast, mineral water, and blankets with us. As darkness fell Nandor and I slipped into one of the coal cars. We had to dig down deep into the coals to sit up. The majority of the time we just lay down and prayed. The coal car was about 50 to 65 feet (15 to 20 m) in length. There were two doors in the middle of the car where the coal was loaded up. There were two small windows with grates. The coal was packed to within $1\frac{1}{2}$ to $2\frac{1}{2}$ feet ($\frac{1}{2}$ to $\frac{3}{4}$ m) of the ceiling. My brother and I were on one side of the car, and my cousin's family were on the other side. We couldn't see my cousin's family because the heap of coal blocked our view.

We left on a Wednesday. On Friday the train stopped. Other material was being loaded onto the train. From the other side of the car, I heard my relatives talking. The husband felt he could not stand it anymore. He was starting to panic and said he was leaving. I tried to calm him down. If he left now he would be caught for sure. They would search the train, and we too would be caught. I whispered, "Have faith, we will be in Switzerland in no time." Somehow he calmed down.

The train started moving again on Monday morning. We had been on the train for nine days when it stopped once more.

That morning my brother had a dream. He saw my mother sitting down beside him, reassuring him that everything would be all right. It was not until much later that we discovered our mother had already been murdered. My brother had felt her presence in that dark coal train with us.

Later that day, the door of our compartment was opened. A flashlight, held by a German officer, was shining on our blackened faces. I motioned to my brother to be quiet. The Nazi said that he smelled people in our compartment. He said he was coming back. We lay in the dark coals for hours contemplating our death. We figured he was getting more officers and dogs. Another couple of hours later, the train started to move. Wherever my mother was, she was watching out for us.

After eleven days on the train we finally made it to Switzerland. When we climbed out of our hiding place, the Swiss could not believe their eyes! Somehow we all had escaped to safety.

Between April and June 1940, the German forces invaded Norway, Denmark, Belgium, the Netherlands, Luxembourg, and France. The war was escalating in 1941. The German forces also invaded Yugo-slavia and Greece. On January 20, 1942, the Wannsee Conference was held by the Nazi authorities to plan the Final Solution to rid the world of the Jews. Germany was winning the war, and Hitler's Final Solution went into effect. No Jew in the occupied territories was safe.

Renata

Renata and her mother lived in her grandmother's house, which the police had just visited. She and her mother knew that it was no longer safe for them to return there.

I reluctantly left my grandmother in Zagreb and traveled quickly to meet my mother at her friend's house outside the city. The people were very frightened and said we could stay only one night.

My mother had befriended the German commander of the factory where she worked. He was like an Oskar Schindler to us, a non-Jew who saved the lives of many Jewish employees in his factory. I always fancied that he was in love with my mother. On the other hand, very few people could refuse anything my mother requested.

The German commander arranged for us to cross the river in a small rowboat the next night. We were hidden under hay on the boat and then transferred to a cart, where we also hid beneath the hay. We

Background photo: The Chamber of Deputies in occupied Paris bears the German victory sign and flies the Nazi flag.

arrived and stayed just a short time at the home of a prosperous farmer. The German commander then picked us up in a big car and told everyone that he was taking us to the hospital for an operation. We then disappeared from Zagreb. It was October 1941. We stayed in Ljubljana. It was occupied by the Italians. We waited to be transferred to Italy. We did not have too much money. We survived in an attic room. I remember roaming the city and standing in long lines waiting for bread.

In February 1942 we were relocated to the village of Mel, Italy, not far from Venice. For the time being we were safe. My mother wanted to be reunited with my father and brother. She started bothering the Italian officials to let us be together. In the meantime, she was concerned about what was happening in Austria, just north of us. She thought that the Germans on the border were too close for comfort. She came to a major decision: her family was not safe in Mel. About twenty Jews from Zagreb were living in Mel at that time. My mother urged them all to leave. They refused to listen to her. During the war all but two were murdered.

She persistently bothered the Italian officials, and they eventually transferred us to the town nearest the Swiss border, Merate. There we were tearfully reunited with my father and brother.

In September 1943, my mother had another premonition. She became afraid in Merate and decided that we should all leave by climbing over the Alps into Switzerland.

Renata in Merate, Italy, November 15, 1943.

Before we could get out, the Germans came looking for Jews in the town. It was such a small town. Everyone knew we were hiding there. Anyone in town could have turned us in to the Germans. My mother, father, brother, and cousins hid in the hay fields while I hid at a friend's house. No one in that little town turned us in. The whole town protected us even while knowing that if we had been caught, they would probably have had to pay the price for hiding us with their own lives.

In late September, we left and climbed over the Alps. I was young but for the older people in our group climbing a mountain was exhausting. I helped as best I could but I could not take away the fear.

We finally made it to the Swiss border. The young guard on duty would not let us in because we were Jews and had no passports or papers. My mother stood her ground and told him, "Shoot us. We are not leaving." She was not well. She had been suffering from hepatitis

Below: The Swiss Alps viewed from Grindelwald, Switzerland.

and had just finished climbing the Alps. But she stood firm. Somehow her fierce determination won out again, and we were allowed to enter Switzerland. We were finally free.

Many Jewish refugees were not allowed to enter Switzerland. But a police officer by the name of Paul Grinninger was in charge of the Swiss Border Police near St. Gallen. He disobeyed orders and allowed a great number of Jews to cross illegally into Switzerland. He and others like him saved many lives.

Renata, her cousin, a friend, and Renata's brother in Merate, Italy, 1943.

Sam

Sam reached southern France in 1940. He was a soldier of the Polish army in temporarily demobilized status and worked in labor camps in the unoccupied part of France. In August 1942, the French, by arrangement with the Germans, started rounding up the Jews and sending them to death camps. It became apparent that Jews would not be protected.

The head of Sam's group, a Polish captain, came to him one day. He said that he had inside information that all the Jews in southern France were going to be rounded up that night. It was time for Sam to escape once more.

I was glad that I had great faith in the Polish leader's information. I knew that being caught by the Germans meant deportation. As it became dark, I escaped into the woods and hid in a farmer's barn. I was ready to fight. I would not be caught! It was a long, long night. I had heard that the Swiss border was now closed to Jews. I knew that I had to go to Spain. Two other Jews were hiding in the barn with me. One chose to go with me. The other stayed. The one who stayed was turned in and murdered. I was lucky again!

The only way to get to Spain was by crossing the Pyrenees. The lowest peaks of the mountains ranged from 3,000 to 4,000 feet. My friend and I started climbing at the lower section of the mountain range. There was always the concern of the Nazis patrolling the area, so we climbed higher and higher. We followed the dried-up river paths. If there had been a flash flood from a sudden storm, we would have been killed instantly. The risks were great. We sometimes had to creep on our hands and knees to climb the mountains. We ran out of food and ate wild grapes.

Finally, after a week, we descended. We were hungry, and our hands and knees were scraped, but we had made it to Spain. We walked as far as Barbastro, a small town, which had a railway station. We bought tickets to travel in the direction of Madrid. I desperately wanted to eat a banana, and with the little money I had I enjoyed some food and this precious piece of fruit.

A policeman (Guardia Civil) spotted us at the train station and thought we looked suspicious as we were strangers. We had no papers. We were interrogated as to what we had seen when we crossed the mountains. I told the truth. All I had seen were a shepherd and his dogs.

We were sent to an internment camp, Miranda de Ebro, that interned foreigners in Spain. I wanted to go to England to fight. I was interned until spring 1943. I was never treated badly. It could have been much worse. If I had remained in Poland, Belgium, or France I would not have survived.

I was released with other Polish soldiers, as arranged by a representative of the Polish government in exile. We went to Madrid.

After a few months we took a train to Portugal. I fell asleep in the last car of the train. When I woke up I discovered that the last car had been disconnected from one train and reconnected to another. Where was I going now? My new destination was the Rock of Gibraltar. In a Royal Navy motorboat in the middle of the night I arrived at my new destination. We were finally outside of German-run Europe!

I loved the feeling of Gibraltar. I felt liberated. There were monkeys everywhere, and their playful antics restored my faith. There was a local Sephardic synagogue on Gibraltar, and I was honored during a Saturday-morning service. It was a very spiritual feeling to pray again with other Jews. In August 1943 I landed in England. I was now ready to fight. I continued in the Polish army and was eventually transferred by request to the British army.

At the end of 1944 I was traveling again, this time to India as a soldier in the British army. I was there at the historic moment when Germany was defeated. The war in Europe was finally over!

My prayers were answered: my sister Regine had survived. She had been put on a transport train in 1942 and had literally walked off it. Regine could have been shot instantly. But she had been determined to survive and took the risk. She escaped and was hidden by a Polish family. She then traveled to Germany and worked under false papers as a non-Jew. After the war ended we were reunited in Belgium. Regine and I were the only ones from our family who escaped.

Sam and Regine, 1930.

chapter five

What It Means to Have Escaped the Holocaust

Those who managed to escape the maze of Nazi persecution—like Helga Edelstein Stummer, Leopold Mendlovic, Renata Markovic Eisen, and Sam Cukier—are proof that even in the most terrible of situations one can still have hope of finding a solution, a way out. Some will say they survived out of sheer luck. Some will say it was by divine intervention. When you read the stories of their lives you may wonder, Could I do the same?

Today, Helga, a grandmother, is involved in the Kindertransport Group, an organization with survivors from all over the world. Most lost their families in the Holocaust. Many were orphaned at young ages. There is a strong connection between those who were on the Kindertranports even to this day.

Helga did not fulfill her dream of killing Hitler, but she did overcome him by staying alive. She tries to fill the world with love and caring in her daily life, one person at a time. To her, hatred has to be eliminated. The sound of children's carefree laughter reminds her of her mother and what could have been if she, too, had experienced a childhood without fear.

Leopold has been blessed with two children and six grandchildren. He has always kept in touch with his remaining five surviving brothers and sisters. No pictures of his parents remain. He wishes he could have had just one to show his children and grandchildren.

From her love of travel, Renata became a travel agent. She is proud of her two children and four grandchildren. Her mother died more than ten years ago. Her mother never stopped weeping for her oldest son. She always felt guilty that she couldn't save his life. She saved so many lives, including Renata's.

Renata feels that she is alive due to her mother's instincts. Her mother protected her. She still remembers the book *The Boys from Paul Street*. For her the bullies were the Germans, and what they killed was her youth.

Sam is happily married and has one daughter. He speaks seven languages and can read nine. Sam is earning another degree in history at the University of Toronto. He is already a chemist. He recently received an award from the president of the University of Toronto for his high marks.

Max and Helga Stummer.

At the awards reception, most people were surprised to see someone seventy-six years of age receiving the award. In Sam's heart, he knew that his parents were with him and watching his success. They had always thought that education was everything. Sam has never stopped learning.

When people ask the question, "Can the Holocaust happen again?" Sam, who studies history, answers, "People have killed each other from the beginning of time. The cycle has never ended. But, most important, individuals always have escaped and survived."

No one wants to think that the Holocaust could happen again: that a nation would isolate one group of people, take away all of their rights, and murder them systematically with the most

Leopold's daughter, son-in-law, and six grandchildren.

advanced technology available. Hatred and prejudice still exist around the world. But there is also hope that injustice will not be overlooked now or in the future as it was then.

Helga, Leopold, Renata, and Sam all received help from others. From family members to non-Jews, even to whole towns, people assisted the four along their journeys to freedom. At any time they each could have been one of the 6 million Jews who were murdered. The courage of these four, combined with the courage of those who were willing to help them, allowed them to live.

From the moment they entered the maze, there was no turning back. These four escaped to freedom.

Timeline

January 30, 1933	Adolf Hitler is appointed chancellor of Germany.
March 23, 1933	Dachau, the first concentration camp, is built to hold political opponents of Nazis.
April 1, 1933	Nazis proclaim a daylong boycott of Jewish-owned businesses.
July 14, 1933	Nazis outlaw all other political parties in Germany; a law is passed legalizing forced sterilization of Roma and Sinti (Gypsies), mentally and physically disabled Germans, African-Germans, and others.
January 26, 1934	Germany and Poland sign Non-Aggression Pact.
August 1, 1935	"No Jews" signs appear in Germany forbidding Jews from stores, restaurants, places of entertainment, etc.
September 15, 1935	German parliament passes the Nuremberg Laws.
March 13, 1938	Germany annexes Austria.
September 29, 1938	Munich Conference: Britain and France allow Hitler to annex part of Czechoslovakia in order to prevent war.
November 9, 1938	*Kristallnacht* (looting and vandalism of Jewish homes businesses and wholesale destruction of synagogues) occurs throughout Germany and Austria; 30,000 Jews are sent to Nazi concentration camps.
March 15, 1939	Germany invades all of Czechoslovakia.
August 23, 1939	Germany and Soviet Union sign Non-Aggression Pact.
September 1, 1939	Germany invades western Poland.
September 2, 1939	Great Britain and France declare war on Germany.
September 17, 1939	Soviet Union invades eastern Poland.

Spring 1940	Germany invades Denmark, Norway, Holland, Luxembourg, Belgium, and France.
March 24, 1941	Germany invades North Africa.
April 6, 1941	Germany invades Yugoslavia and Greece.
June 22, 1941	Germany invades western Soviet Union.
July 31, 1941	Reinhard Heydrich appointed to carry out the "Final Solution" (extermination of all European Jews).
Summer 1941	*Einsatzgruppen* (mobile killing squads) begin to massacre Jews in western Soviet Union.
December 7, 1941	Japan bombs Pearl Harbor; United States enters World War II.
January 20, 1942	Wannsee Conference: Nazi leaders meet to design "Final Solution."
Spring and Summer 1942	Many Polish ghettos emptied; residents deported to death camps.
February 2, 1943	German troops in Stalingrad, Soviet Union, surrender; the Allies begin to win the war.
June 11, 1943	Nazis decide that all ghettos in Poland and Soviet Union are to be emptied and residents deported to death camps.
March 19, 1944	Germany occupies Hungary.
June 6, 1944	D-Day: Normandy Invasion by the Allies.
May 8, 1945	Germany surrenders to the Allies; war ends in Europe.

Glossary

Alps The largest mountain range in Europe.

annex To incorporate a territory within the domain of a state.

antisemitism Hatred toward or bias against the Jewish people.

Aryan According to Nazi ideology, a person of Nordic or Germanic background, a member of Hitler's "master race."

Auschwitz-Birkenau A Nazi death camp near Cracow, Poland, where more than 2 million Jews were murdered.

concentration camp A camp where people are kept in inhumane conditions, and are killed by starvation, exhaustion, disease, or execution.

cosmopolitan International and sophisticated.

death camp A camp set up to kill people and dispose of their bodies.

democratic Concerning government ruled by the people.

Final Solution The term used by Nazis for their systematic plan to murder the entire Jewish population of Europe.

ghetto A part of a city set aside by the Nazis to contain only Jews, which was heavily guarded and lacking in food, water, heat, housing, and health care.

Holocaust A period (1939–1945) in which 6 million Jews perished under the Nazis.

immigration The act of moving to one country after having left another.

integrated The condition of being part of something.

Judenrein German for "free of Jews."

Kristallnacht The Nazi-organized demonstration of violence against the Jews of Germany and Austria on the night of November 9, 1938.

Nazi The political party that ruled in Germany (1933–1945); full name: National Socialist German Workers' Party.

Nuremberg Laws German laws passed on September 15, 1935, that legalized antisemitism and stripped Jewish Germans of many rights.

observant Obeying religious law and tradition.

Orthodox Judaism The religion of those who adhere most strictly to Jewish traditional beliefs and practices.

ostracize To exclude or banish.

premonition A warning of danger ahead of time.

propaganda Ideas, usually biased, that are spread intentionally to promote a cause or to damage an opposing cause.

Pyrenees A mountain range separating France from Spain.

quarantine A period of isolation so that infection will not spread.

refuge A place of safety to which a person goes to escape danger.

secular Not religious.

Shabbat Sabbath; the Jewish day of rest, from sundown on Friday until sundown on Saturday.

shtetl A small Jewish town or village.

synagogue A Jewish house of worship.

Treblinka A Nazi death camp near Treblinka, Poland, where approximately 840,000 Jews were murdered.

Wannsee Conference The meeting at which plans for the "Final Solution" were discussed by the Nazis; held on January 20, 1942, in Berlin, Germany.

Warsaw Ghetto Uprising A twenty-eight-day revolt that occurred in the Warsaw Ghetto, an area in Warsaw, Poland, in which approximately 500,000 Jews were brutally confined by the Nazis. The ghetto was gradually emptied as inhabitants were secretly sent to death camps. The revolt occurred when many of the approximately 56,000 remaining ghetto inhabitants resisted Nazi plans to send them to death camps.

World War I The war in Europe that lasted from 1914 until 1918.

World War II The most devastating war in human history, it lasted from 1939 until 1945 and involved countries all over the world.

Zionist movement A movement begun in the nineteenth century to promote the return of Jews to their homeland in the Land of Israel.

For Further Reading

Altschuler, David A. *Hitler's War Against the Jews—The Holocaust: A Young Reader's Version of the War Against the Jews: 1933–1945 by Lucy Dawidowicz.* West Orange, NJ: Behrman House, 1978.

Drucker, Malka, and Michael Halperin. *Jacob's Rescue: A Holocaust Story.* New York: Bantam Doubleday Dell, 1993.

Eisenberg, Azriel. *The Lost Generation: Children in the Holocaust.* New York: Pilgrim Press, 1982.

Eliach, Yaffa. *Hasidic Tales of the Holocaust.* New York: Random House, 1988.

Frank, Anne. *Diary of a Young Girl: The Definitive Edition.* New York: Doubleday, 1995.

Holliday, Laurel. *Children in the Holocaust and World War II: Their Secret Diaries.* New York: Washington Square Press, 1994.

Klein, Gerda. *All but My Life.* New York: Hill & Wang, 1995.

Marks, Jane. *The Hidden Children: The Secret Survivors of the Holocaust.* New York: Ballantine Books, 1993.

Matas, Carol. *Daniel's Story.* New York: Simon and Schuster, 1996.

Rochman, Hazel, and Darlene Z. McCampbell, eds. *Bearing Witness: Stories of the Holocaust.* New York: Orchard Books/Watts, 1995.

Roth-Hano, Renee. *Touch Wood*. New York: Puffin Books, 1989.

Tec, Nechama. *Dry Tears: The Story of a Lost Childhood*. New York: Oxford University Press, 1984.

Wiesel, Elie. *Night*. New York: Bantam Books, 1982.

Wilkomirski, Benjamin. *Fragments*. New York: Schocken Books, 1996.

For Advanced Readers

Bauer, Yehuda. *A History of the Holocaust*. New York: Franklin Watts.

Baumel, Judith Tydor. *Unfulfilled Promise: Rescue and Resettlement of Jewish Refugee Children in the United States, 1934–1945*. Juneau, Alaska: Denali Press 1990.

Berenbaum, Michael. *The World Must Know*. Boston: Little, Brown, 1993.

Dwork, Deborah. *Children with a Star*. New Haven, Conn.: Yale University Press, 1991.

Friedman, Ina R.. *Escape or Die: True Stories of Young People Who Survived the Holocaust*. Cambridge, Mass.: Yellow Moon, 1991.

I Never Saw Another Butterfly: Children's Drawings and Poems from Theresienstadt Concentration Camp. New York: McGraw-Hill, 1964.

Noakes, J., and G. Pridham. *Nazism: A History in Documents and Eyewitness Accounts, Vols. I and II*. New York: Pantheon Books, 1984.

Videos

The Courage to Care
The film features ordinary people who refused to accept Nazi tyranny and reached out to help victims of the Holocaust. (Available from Zenger Video, 10200 Jefferson Boulevard, Room 902, P. O. Box 802, Culver City, CA 90232-0802; (800) 421-4246.)

The Double Crossing: The Voyage of the St. Louis
This film explores the tragic fate of the passengers on the *S.S. St. Louis* who attempted to flee to Cuba. (Available from Zenger Video, 10200 Jefferson Boulevard, Room 902, P. O. Box 802, Culver City, CA 90232-0802; (800) 421-4246.)

More Than Broken Glass: Memories of Kristallnacht
Using archival footage and photographs and interviews with survivors, this video explores the persecution of Jews in Germany before and during the Holocaust. (Available from Ergo Media, Inc., P. O. Box 2037, Teaneck, NJ 07666; (800) 695-3746.)

Raoul Wallenberg: Between the Lines
Friends, family, and former members of Wallenberg's staff describe his efforts to confront the Nazi destruction of Hungarian Jewry. (Available from Social Studies School Services, 10200 Jefferson Boulevard, Room J, P. O. Box 802, Culver City, CA 90232-0802; (800) 421-4246.)

Safe Haven
This video profiles America's only refugee camp for victims of Nazi terror. Nearly 1,000 refugees were brought to Oswego, NY, and incarcerated in a camp known as Fort Ontario for eighteen months. (Available from the Anti-Defamation League, 823 United Nations Plaza, New York, NY 10017; (212) 885-7700.)

Shoah
This film includes interviews with victims, perpetrators, and bystanders, and takes viewers to camps, towns, and railways that were part of the Holocaust. (Available in most video stores and many libraries.)

Web Sites

Anti-Defamation League—Braun Holocaust Institute
http://www.adl.org/Braun/braun.htm

Holocaust Education and Memorial Centre of Toronto
http://www.feduja.org

Museum of Tolerance
www.wiesenthal.com/mot/index.html

Simon Wiesenthal Center
http://www.wiesenthal.com/

United States Holocaust Memorial Museum
http://www.ushmm.org/index.html

Yad Vashem
http://www.yad-vashem.org.il

Index

About the Author

Sandra Giddens is currently completing her doctorate of education at the University of Toronto. She has been a teacher for more than twenty years, specializing in special education. She is currently doing educational assessments. The author grew up in Toronto with her mother, father, brother, and sister. She lives with her loving family: husband, Owen; daughter, Justine; and son, Kyle.

The author's research on the Holocaust began in 1994 when she was an interviewer for the Shoah Foundation project established by Steven Spielberg. Giddens has written poems about the Holocaust, a number of which have been published. She strongly believes that the Holocaust must never be forgotten: each generation needs to teach the next generation so that history will not repeat itself.

About the Series Editor

Yaffa Eliach is Professor of History and Literature in the Department of Judaic Studies at Brooklyn College. She founded and directed the Center for Holocaust Studies (now part of the Museum of Jewish Heritage—A Living Memorial to the Holocaust) and designed the Tower of Life exhibit at the U.S. Holocaust Memorial Museum. Professor Eliach is the author of *Hasidic Tales of the Holocaust; We Were Children Just Like You; There Once Was a World: A Nine Century Chronicle of the Shtetl of Eishyshok;* and *The Liberators: Eyewitness Accounts of the Liberation of Concentration Camps.*

Photo Credits

Cover photo courtesy of Helga Edelstein Stummer; pp. 6–7, 19, 50 courtesy of Sam Cukier; p. 8 © Leni Sonnenfeld, courtesy of the United States Holocaust Memorial Museum (USHMM) Photo Archives; pp. 10, 22, 24–25, 29, 30 © National Archives, courtesy of USHMM Photo Archives; pp. 10 (background), 12 (both), 40, 52 courtesy of Helga Edelstein Stummer; pp. 11, 35, 37 © Main Commission for the Investigation of Nazi War Crimes, courtesy of USHMM Photo Archives; p. 13 © Inge Eisenstaedt, courtesy of USHMM Photo Archives; pp. 14, 53 courtesy of Leopold Mendlovic; pp. 15, 23 © courtesy of Yad Vashem Jerusalem; p. 16–17 © YIVO Institute for Jewish Research, courtesy of USHMM Photo Archives; pp. 18, 33, 46, 48 courtesy of Renata Eisen; pp. 20, 28, 30–31 © courtesy of USHMM Photo Archives; p. 21 (both) © Morris Rosen Collection, courtesy of USHMM Photo Archives; p. 26 © Dwight D. Eisenhower Library, courtesy of USHMM Photo Archives; p. 27 © Betty Troper Yaeger Collection, courtesy of USHMM Photo Archives; p. 32 © Archiwum Akt Nowych, courtesy of USHMM Photo Archives; p. 34–35 © Philip Vock, courtesy of USHMM Photo Archives; pp. 36, 41, 42, 44–45, 47 © courtesy of Archive Photos; p. 43 © KZ Gedenkstatte Dachau, courtesy of USHMM Photo Archives; p. 43 (background) © Muzeum Okregowe Knoin, courtesy of USHMM Photo Archives; pp. 38–39 Frances Rose Collection, courtesy of USHMM Photo Archives.

Series Design
Kim Sonsky

Layout
Laura Murawski